Other Titles by *Langaa* RPCIG

Francis B Nyamnjoh
Stories from Abakwa
Mind Searching
The Disillusioned African
The Convert
Souls Forgotten

Dibussi Tande
No Turning Back. Poems of Freedom 1990-1993

Kangsen Feka Wakai
Fragmented Melodies

Ntemfac Ofege
Namondo. Child of the Water Spirit

Emmanuel Fru Doh
Not Yet Damascus
The Fire Within

Thomas Jing
Tale of an African Woman

Peter Wuteh Vakunta
Grassfields Stories from Cameroon
Cry My Beloved Africa

Ba'bila Mutia
Coils of Mortal Flesh

Kehbuma Langmia
Titabet and The Takumbeng

Ngessimo Mathe Mutaka

TEFL ... es as ... cy tools

Cameroon's Social Democratic Front: Its History and Prospects as an Opposition Political party, 1990-2011

Sammy Oke Akombi
The Raped Amulet
The Woman Who Ate Python

Susan Nkwentie Nde
Precipice

Francis B Nyamnjoh & Richard Fonteh Akum
The Cameroon GCE Crisis: A Test of Anglophone Solidarity

Joyce Ashuntantang & Dibussi Tande
Their Champagne Party Will End! Poems in Honor of Bate Besong

Rosemary Ekosso
House of Falling Women

Mwalimu George Ngwane
The Power in the Writer: Collected Essays on Culture, Development and Democracy in Africa

GREEN RAPE
Poetry For The Environment

Peter Wuteh Vakunta

Langaa Research & Publishing CIG
Mankon, Bamenda

Publisher:
Langaa RPCIG
(*Langaa* Research & Publishing Common Initiative Group)
P.O. Box 902 Mankon
Bamenda
North West Province
Cameroon
Langaagrp@gmail.com
www.langaapublisher.com

ISBN:9956-558-48-6

© Peter Vakunta 2008
First Published 2008

DISCLAIMER
All views expressed in this publication are those of the author and do not necessarily reflect the views of Langaa RPCIG.

DEDICATION

In memory of the victims of Tsunami and Katrina

Many a man lives a burden to the earth; but a good book is the precious life-blood of a master spirit, embalmed and treasured up on purpose to a life beyond life *[Milton]*

Acknowledgement

Most of the poems presented here have been published before as work in progress. I thank the publishers of the following publications for permission to include them in the present volume: *Earth Love*, U.K; *Linkway*, U.K.; *New Authors Journal*, U.S.A; *Offerings*, U.S.A; Creative *Communication*, U.S.A; *International Library of Poetry*, U.S.A; and *Unique Publications*, South Africa. Finally, I would like to express gratitude to all my students, past and present, whose constructive criticisms have helped me hone these poems.

Table of Contents

Foreword

Green Rape: Poetry for the Environment is an anthology of poems written in strong support of environmental literacy. Each poem is the poet's cry of protest against the rape of natural and built environments. The anthology examines a wide range of issues including the clash of global capitalism with environmental activism. It takes a close look at the major themes in international discourse on environmental degradation, climate change, renewable energy sources, global warming, Gene technology, biodiversity and more. The poet dispels a number of myths, notably the existence of an inexhaustible bank of natural resources at the disposal of Man. He attempts to provide a solution to the abusive and unbalanced utilization of scarce natural resources. In a unique way, the poems contribute to the fostering of environmental awareness that would contribute to the sustainable management of natural resources. The poet invites us to look beyond the doomsday rhetoric about the state of the environment and to commit more of our resources where they will do the most good to lifting the world's population out of poverty. The significance of this anthology to environmental education resides in its contribution to the debate on global sustainable development, especially efforts to protect the environment and eradicate poverty.

PART ONE
Free Verse

Cataclysms

Natural disasters/
Like Tsunami and Katrina/
Serve as great reminders/
To all and sundry/
That we live/
On a fragile ecosystem/
Where the tragedy of One/
Is tantamount to
the calamity of All/
Tragedy of the Commons/

Earth Poem

You'd be surprised/
how many people don't know/
that the Earth's ecosystem is fragile/
That's because they don't know/
that the ecosystem is a fragile web/

It's amazing/
how many people don't know/
that natural resources are exhaustible/
That's because they don't know/
that many of earth's/
resources are non-renewable/

It's mind boggling/
how many people don't know/
that some of earth's species/
are on the brink of extinction/
That's because they don't know/
that the earth harbors/
a myriad endangered species/

It's unbelievable/
how many people don't know/
that Earth's biodiversity/
needs protection/
That's because they don't know/
that human and physical environments/
enjoy reciprocity/

It's unimaginable/
how many people don't know/
that human beings and the natural/
world are on a collision course/
That's because they don' know/
that Man's activities inflict/
irreparable damage on Mother Earth/
Causing climate change/
Aggravating global warming/

It's unfathomable/
how many people don't know/
that it's incumbent on/
the present generation/
to meet its needs without/
compromising the ability/
of future generations/
to meet their own needs/
That's because they don't know/
that we're answerable to posterity/

Ecotage

Wondering what this Lexis stands for? /
Denotes environmental terrorism/
Yeah!
We're environmental terrorists/
We brutalize Mother Earth! /
Scorch her/
Pollute her/
Suffocate her/
Poison her/
Slash her/
Burn her/
Slice her/
Bruise her/
We're a killer nation! /

It is an eyesore/
Streets and parks/
littered with cans, paper/
bottles, wrappings/
Aquatic life a-choking with litter/
Oil spills/
Toxic waste/
Plastics/
Sewage/
And more/

Biodiversity on the/
brink of extinction/
Wild life endangered/
Guess what this generation will/
bequeath to posterity? /
A depleted ecosystem! /
Halt this genocide! /

Animal Beings

There are great words/
in the animal kingdom/
One of such words is/
"Thanks"/

There are weighty words/
in the animal world/
Two of such words are/
"Forgive me"/

There are meaningful words/
in the animal lingo/
Three of such words are/
"I love you"/

One wonders if human beings/
Will ever learn to talk/
like animal beings/

Symbiosis

Animal beings are born/
In all shapes and sizes/
Some small; others big/
Some fat; others lean/
Some tamed; others wild/
We must recognize and nurture/
the different species/
in the animal kingdom/

Animals look different/
in the most part because/
they are endowed with different/
combinations of intelligences/

Humankind should nurse/
the conviction that we would/
have a better world to live in/
if human beings lived in
perfect symbiosis/
With one another like our/
animal friends do/

Mosquito

Nwing! Nwing!
Nocturnal songster
Nwing! Nwing!
Solitary chorister
Nwing! Nwing!
Avaricious bloodsucker/
Nwing! Nwing!
Ubiquitous sleep snatcher/
Nwing! Nwing!
Creature so invisible
Yet so visible
Nwing! Nwing!
Friend or foe
of the human ear?
Nwing! Nwing!
Vector of human fear
Nwing! Nwing!
Conduit for malaria
Nwing! Nwing!
Harbinger of insomnia/
Nwing! Nwing!
Insect so taciturn
Yet so loquacious
Nwing! Nwing!
He that loathes the mosquito
Undoubtedly loves slumber
Nwing! Nwing!
Mosquito/
Persona non grata/
In slumberland/
Nwing! Nwing!

Eco-Terrorism

Warfare and a healthy planet/
Are incompatible/
The human species/
has gone into overdrive/
On a growth-obsessed path/
Each year 27,000 species go extinct/
Fresh water sources dry up/
Microscopic organisms/
that fertilize soil/
are humus eradicated/

Environmental rights and human/
rights are inseparable/
The ozone hole/
The greenhouse effect/
The extinction of biodiversity/
And the precarious depletion/
Of the earth are interwoven/

Earth's Early Tenants

Every geographic entity/
Has its native people/
The Australoid/
Aborigines of Australia/
Nomadic people comprising/
tribes and clans/

The Maori/
Aborigines of New Zealand/
Native people co-habiting/
with the Pakeha whites/

The San (Bushmen)
Autochthonous people/
Of Southern Africa/
Inhabitants of/
The Kalahari Desert/

The Sioux/
Aboriginal peoples/
Of North America/
Living on the reservations/
They're a nation/
With the Nation/

The Pygmies/
Aboriginal tribes of/
Equatorial Africa/
And of South-east Asia/
Leading an arboreal life/

S.O.S
Touche pas à mes potes![1] /
Save the world's indigenous peoples/

---

[1] Leave my friends alone!

Animal Rights

All animals are born equal/
With inalienable rights/
None is more equal/
than the other/
As one animal is born/
so is the other/
As one animal dies/
So dies the other/

All animals breathe the same air/
The same blood runs through their veins/
They defecate in the same manner/
And urinate in the same way/

In coitus/
They assume the same posture/
No animal has an edge over the other/
There are no greater animals/
Neither are they lesser ones/
They are all in the same boat/

Snake Sanctuary

This earth/
is a snake sanctuary/
replete with serpents of all/
shapes and colors/

Rattlesnake/
poisonous snake of America/
Offspring of the viperadae family/

Viper/
venomous snake/
born to the viperadae family/

Python/
constricting snake/
of the pythonidae family/
Boa constrictor/
large nonpoisonous snake/
native to tropical America/
and the West Indies/

Fer-de-lance snake/
highly venomous snake
native to Central America/
And South America/

Anaconda/
Enormous nonpoisonous aquatic snake/
With such a multitude of serpents/
How can one play safe?/

Brotherhood of the Jungle

I am not a loner/
My siblings are legion/
Lion/
King of the jungle/
Tiger/
Fierce energetic brother/
Leopard/
black-potted cousin/
Rhinoceros/
Thick-skinned plant-eating nephew/
Elephant/
Gigantic uncle with a trunk/
And long curved ivory tusks/
Buffalo/
Aunt with backswept horns/
Giraffe/
Tall niece with a long neck/
Cheetah/
Swift-running sister/
with a spotted coat/
Gorilla/
Large-mouthed stepsister with/
a large head and short neck/
Monkey/
Mischievous mimicking grandma/
Jaguar/
Choppy flesh-eating grandpa/
Baboon/
Uncouth stepbrother with a nude butt! /

Kola Nut

He that brings kola/
Brings life,
Quips an illustrious/
son of the soil/

Kola nut/
African Viagra!

Kola nut/
Source of much needed energy/
Energy to work/
Energy to walk/
Energy to talk/
Energy to drink/
Energy to think/
Energy to dance/
Energy to bounce/
Energy to run/

Kola nut/
Benevolent Companion/
In fair weather/
And inclement weather/
Ingredient in pouring libation/
Part and parcel of our *lobola*[2]/
Pacifier in times of disputes/
Kola nut/
Bedfellow well met! /

[2] bride price

Canine Wisdom

Infinitesimal some animals are/
And yet extremely sagacious/
Ants/
Creatures of little strength/
Yet they're able to store up/
Food in abundance in the summer/

Coneys/
Creatures of little power/
Yet they're able to make/
homes in the crags/

Locusts/
Tiny insects with no king to lead them/
Still they're able to advance/
in rank and file/

Lizards/
So small they can be buried/
in the palm of the hand/
Yet they're able to/
inhabit kings' palaces! /
These four are the Sages/
of the animal kingdom/

Biodome

The time is 9:00 a.m. /
The temperature 65°F. /
The date is June 13, 2002/
The place Montreal-Canada/

I am in a biodome/
devoid of freedom/
for my four-legged friends/
There is utter pandemonium/
I am surrounded by a troop/
Of elated elementary and middle kids/
Curious visitors from/
all nooks and crannies/
There is nondescript hysteria/
Some jumping and yelling/
others are stooping and filming/

Here I am in a canine dungeon/
meant to steal the freedom/
of man's valued companions/
amphibians/
mammals/
fishes/
reptiles/
birds/

I stare in utter bewilderment/
at this self-styled natural habitat/
wondering what these creatures/
must be saying to one another/
in the face of human invasion/
I can't help but yell/
Injustice done unto one/
is injustice done unto all/

Genocide

It is the apocalypse! /
A catastrophe has befallen/
Our friends on four/
Some are being slaughtered/
Others are guinea pigs/
In human laboratories/
Some more are being shipped/
to alien lands under the most/
horrendous conditions/

There's pandemonium everywhere/
in the animal kingdom/
Broken bones abound/
Plucked feathers galore/
Who's behind the Genocide? /

McDonald/
Culprit number one/
Subway,
Culprit number two/
Kentucky Fried Chicken/
Culprit number three/
You know the rest/

The cry of animal rights activists/
has fallen on deaf ears! /
This is the voice of the voiceless! /

Grass

So green/
And yet so brown/
Grass/
So short/
And yet so tall/

Grass/
Pregnant with meaning/
A myriad aphorisms/
spin around grass/
Grass is always greener
over the septic tank/

To let grass grow under
your feet is to procrastinate/
He that has fallen
from grace to grass/
has suffered disgrace/

A green snake in
the grass is a foe/
Not a friend! /
Before warned is
before armed—
Dry grass should never
play with fire/

Birds of a Feather

We're birds of a feather/
That flock together/
for better or for worse/
A bird in hand/
Is worth two in the bush/
Yet one swallow does not
make a summer/
There is power
in numbers/
Let's save our
winged friends/

To pose the trifling question
as to who's worthier than who
in the bird kingdom/
is to resume the irksome
chicken-and-egg polemic/
The one is as worthy
as the other/
Let's save our winged friends/

One Man One Tree

Did you know? /
It takes a single/
unlettered man and
one chain saw to demolish/
an entire forest/
But an entire village/
to plant a single forest? /

Did you know? /
Trees are Man's friends/
indeed our lifeblood/
They have life like we do/
They grow, eat, breathe/
procreate and die like we do/
Our communion with trees
must be symbiotic/
not parasitic/
We need their oxygen/
they absorb our
carbon dioxide/

The more reason
why our modus operandi/
should be one man one tree/

Mother Earth

Tell me Mother/
Where are the beautiful trees
that once stood here? /
Tell me/
Where are the clean rivers
that once flew yonder? /
Tell me Mother/
What happened to the evergreen forests? /

Tell me/
Have the fishes all traveled? /
Where is the tilapia? /
Where is the salmon? /
Where is the crab? /
Where's the jellyfish? /
Where have they all gone? /

Tell me/
Where are the birds? /
Where's the kingfisher? /
Where's the guinea fowl? /
Where's the owl? /
What became of the nightingale? /

Tell me/
Why are our soils so sick? /
The rich soil that once looked so dark/
The dark soil that once looked so rich/

Tell me/
Why is Man killing Mother Earth? /
Why is man so cruel? /
Why is man so uncaring? /
Who'll rescue Mother Earth? /
I want to know! /

Termites

Termites
These insects don't build/
They destroy/
They've destroyed our economies/
They've destroyed our coffee plants.

Termites
These insects don't nurture/
They devastate/
They've destroyed our livelihood/
They've destroyed our palm trees/
They've destroyed our cocoa plants/
They've destroyed our source of income/

Termites
These insects are hard/
at work destroying/
the legacy bequeathed/
to Man by Mother Earth/
Termites are in charge of
our collective destiny/
Shall they make or mar? /
That is the question/
It's time for fumigation! /

Son-Of-The-Soil

I am/
A Son-of-the-Soil/
I pour libation therefore I am/
I am/
A Son-of-the-Soil/

Son-of-the-Soil.
I'm circumcised because
I'm a Son-of-the-Soil.

Son-of-the-Soil/
I attended the
initiation school because/
I'm a Son-of-the-Soil/

Son-of-the-Soil/
I'm a full-fledge member/
Of the *Quifon*³ Society because/
I'm a Son-of-the-Soil/

Son-of-the-Soil/
I beat the *Samba*⁴ drum because/
I'm a Son-of-the-Soil.

Son-of-the-Soil/
I dance the *Manjong*⁵ because/
I'm a Son-of-the-Soil/

Son-of-the-Soil/
I pay the *lobola* because/
I'm a Son-of- the-Soil/

Wherever I go/
Whatever I do/
However I shall be/
I remain a Son-of-the-Soil/

---

³ secret society
⁴ traditional dance
⁵ traditional dance for elders

The Creed

To save the environment/
To restore a sense of balance/
to God's creation/
Humanity needs common sense to halt/
the sins of capitalism/

Thou shall hold nature in awe/
Thou shall not be the ruler of the earth/
Thou shall not be an irrational/
user of earth's scarce resources/
Thou shall not conquer nature for the sole/
purpose of enjoying life/

Let this not be misconstrued/
as an invitation to be a primitive savage/
Harken!
The earth is in the balance/
The onus is on thee to/
keep the balance inviolate/

Guinea Pigs

Man has waged many/
a war against man/
since the dawn of time/
But the mother of all wars/
is gene warfare/

Genetic engineering no longer/
symbolizes merely/
molecules of DNA/
It connotes war-mongering/
In the hands of villains/
inorganic substances/
play a lethal role/
Ponder the anthrax scare! /

Gene tech is the root cause/
of many an ailment/
It disrupts the ecosystem/
depletes biodiversity,
orchestrates soil/
and water pollution/

No one is sure of/
The long-term effects of/
genetic engineering/
on the physical and/
human environments/
Not even the gene engineers! /

The more we speculate/
the more illusory it becomes/
Consider the specter of cloned/
environmental terrorists/

Strains of antibiotic–resistant/
bacteria owe strength to Gene tech/
On agricultural land,
Gene-tech accounts for the disruption
of ecosystems.

Gene-tech eases the depletion of
biodiversity,
Gene-tech creates novel plant diseases,
Gene-tech orchestrates soil pollution,
Gene-tech depletes soil ecology.
Gene-tech, number one
culprit in toxicity.
Gene-tech, catalyst in water pollution,
cancer and birth defects/
We're all guinea pigs! /

Quiet Peace-Makers

I have half a mind to/
turn and live with the birds/
They are forever tranquil/
I watch them in utter admiration/
As they go about their daily chores/
In total tranquility/

They do not rave and rant/
about what tomorrow/
holds in store for them/
They don't anger me/
with tales of lust/

None amasses wealth/
No one builds castles in the air/
None abuses power/
No one exploits the other.
None indulges in debauchery.
Not a single one harbors/
Lustful desires out of season/
They all accept their lot in life/

Campfire

What's this word? /
What's it worth? /
Campfires are welcome/
whenever they come/

Campfires are distractions/
from our daily attractions/
While we bask in/
the warmth of a campfire/
We should never misfire/
by shooting at the live deer/
that lies in good cheer/

The good beer/
ushered by a campfire each day/
should be shared by folks everyday/

Sounds of Nature

How mute would the world/
be without sounds of nature/
Nature is replete with sounds/
Chirping of insects/
Buzzing of bees/
Croaking of frogs/
Hooting of owls/
Whistling of whales/
Crowing of cocks/
Sizzling of snakes/

How silent would the world/
be without sounds of nature/
Nature is full of sounds--
Barking of dogs/
Mooing of cows/
Squeaking of squirrels/
Mewing of cats/
Roaring of lions/
Trumpeting of elephants/
Bleating of goats/

How dead would the world/
be without sounds of nature/
Nature abounds with sounds/
Gushing of water/
Pelting of rain/
Cracking of thunder/
Thundering of the earthquake/

How dumb would this world/
be without sounds/
of nature! /

Beauty In Nature!

There's beauty in nature/
There's happiness in nature/
In the fragrance of flowers/
In the greenery of trees/
In the blue of rivers and streams/

There's beauty in nature/
In the rockiness of mountains/
In the stillness of waters/
In the whiteness of snow/

There's beauty in nature/
In the brownness of the soil/
In the azure of the sky/
In the brightness of the sun/
In the darkness of night/
In the wetness of rain/

There's beauty in nature/
In everything you see in nature/
Go outside and stare/
at the moon/
It's beautiful! /

There's beauty in nature/
Enjoy the colors of the rainbow/
Feel the texture of the air/
Smile at the stars/
Bask in the warmth/
of the sun/
There's beauty in nature! /

Green Rape!

How many more species/
Must go extinct/
Before it dawns on Man/
That he's Earth's worst predator? /

Sing requiem/
for the Dodo/
Sing the dirge/
for the Dinosaur/
Sing the funeral song/
for the White Rhino/
Sing the death song/
for the Black Mamo/
Sing the mourning song/
for the Hawaiian Akialoa/
Sing farewell/
to the Lanai Creeper/
Sing adieu/
to the Amastra Cornea/

Where is the Odynerus Radula? /
Where is the Dinofelis? /
Where is the Metailurus? /
Where is the Smilodon? /
Where is the Megantereon? /

These and many more are/
Lost generations whose demise/
is attributable to Man. /

Ozone

What is this word? /
What does it mean? /
Ozone is a colorless reactive gas/
Each molecule of which contains/
three oxygen atoms/

At high altitude/
these atoms form/
the ozone layer/
thin layer of the stratosphere/
Rampant use of chlorine-based/
substances, chlorofluorocarbons/
and chlorinated solvents orchestrate/
ozone depletion/engendering the ozone hole/

The consequence of the ozone hole/
is not obvious to the untrained eye/
Suffice it to say that before long/
humanity would be grappling/
with skin cancer, cataracts and more/
if nothing is done to halt/
the incessant depletion/
of the ozone layer/

The Big Five

It wasn't so much/
the vast expanse of/
greenery and biotic diversity/
of the Kruger National Park /
or the face-to-face encounter/
with a live elephant that made/
the most impression on my five senses/
Rather it was the nocturnal howls/
Of famished hyenas that made/
my hair stand on end/

The Park is a world on its own/
harboring a myriad organisms/
Some visible/
Others microscopic/
First I saw the buffalo/
then I saw the giraffe/
later the elephant! /

I was dying/
to see the much-acclaimed Big Five: /
Leopard, rhinoceros, lion, buffalo, elephant/
Alas, I ran out of pot-luck/
Nonetheless, a day in the Park/
Is worth a lifetime outside/
It's a real experience! /

Aqua Vitae

Water,
Source of life/
Source of a myriad idioms too! /
To be in deep water/
Is to be in deep trouble/
To be between the devil/
And the deep blue sea/
Is to be on the horns of a dilemma/
Still waters that run deep/
Is a quiet demeanor that/
Conceals depths of cunning/
To cast one's bread upon the waters/
Is to do good without expecting reward/

There's more to water/
than meets the eye/
Like water off a duck's back/
Is said of remonstrance that/
produces no effect/
To make one's mouth water/
Is to whet one's appetite/
stimulate one's anticipation/
Water under the bridge/
Are past events accepted as irrevocable/

A fish out of water/
Is said of a person/
in an unwelcome situation/
To fish in troubled waters/
is to take advantage/
of a bad situation.

Christmas Trees

The Christmas tree is a common sight/
In the homes of Christians at Christmas/
But what do we do with/
the tree after Christmas? /
If you are like most
tree-consumers/
you haul it to the trash/
where it ends up in a landfill/
In the process, you are also tossing/
out a variety of benefits the tree/
can offer after the holidays/

The boughs cut into/
one-to-two foot lengths/
can serve as a kind of blanket against/
harsh winter winds for delicate/
perennials such as azaleas/
camellias and rosebushes/
The pleasant-smelling needles and cones/
can give a piney aroma to a compost heap/
Although, they take somewhat longer/
than other foliage to decompose/
Evergreens will eventually contribute/
to a rich mixture of compost/

Pine and fir needles make/
good soil conditioners, loosening/
and lightening the consistency/
of sandy or clay soils/
The acidic residue they/
give off when they decompose/
is ideal for many plants/
including azaleas and rhododendrons/

The tree trunk can be useful/
in the garden, although you'll/
have to run it through/
a shredder or chipper/
The finished product can be added/
to the soil as mulch or compost/
Be careful about burning/

evergreens in your fireplace/
The heavy concentrations of resin/
increase the risk of chimney fire/
Besides, the wood burns too quickly/
to make for a good fire/

Life-Savers

You may think of trees/
As a gift from Mother Nature/
Something to climb up or sit under/
You probably don't think of
Trees as life-savers/
But that's exactly what they are/

In cities and countryside/
Trees breathe life into our planet/
And save us from a host/
of environmental problems/
Aside from the beauty of trees/
And the food some of them produce/
Trees are helpful in many ways/

Urban areas are 'heat islands'/
Buildings, streets, cars/
and other infrastructure/
And human activities soak up heat/
on summer days and release it at night/
Trees offset this heat/
operating as nature's air conditioners/
Trees also help to reduce/
noise pollution in cities/
Noise pollution/
The great nuisance! /

Trees offer the cheapest way/
To combat the greenhouse effect/
They absorb carbon dioxide
Released into the environment/
By dirty industries/

Carbon dioxide and greenhouse gases
are responsible for global warming/
Big problem facing the global community! /

Trees protect us against/
The erosive power of the wind/
They protect topsoil/
And retain soil moisture/

Deprived of their protective tree cover/
hillsides are easily eroded/
Without trees to break its force/
The wind finds exposed/
topsoil easy pickings/

The shade provided by trees/
saves considerable amounts/
of energy and money/
In the summer/
Trees placed around a house/
can cut home air-conditioning energy/
needs by 10 to 15 percent! /

Green Washing

On Earth Day/
year in year out/
we pay lip service to stewardship/
toward the environment/
The worst despoilers/
make the loftiest speeches/

Yet Our Environmental Policy Act/
is a loud-sounding nothing! /
The Clear Air Act/
not worthier than/
the paper on which it's written/
The Clean Water Act a sham! /
Illegal spills and groundwater/
pollution continues unabated/

We've turned Our backs/
on the Kyoto Protocol/
that seeks to contain global warming/
even though we are the worst global polluters/
We've stalled research/
on alternative energy sources/
Preferring nuclear energy/
to less deleterious energies: /
solar, wind and other forms/
of efficient energy sources/

Our dirty technologies/
are hazardous to physical/
and built environments/
yet we continue to green wash them/
Our Land and Water Conservation Fund/
is a white elephant! /

In the arena of environmentalism/
talk should be backed by action/
It's incumbent upon current tenants/
of the earth to leave to posterity/
a better planet than they inherited/

G-Foods

Boon or Bane? /
Polemics surrounding genetically/
modified foods continue to tear/
the world asunder/
Some trumpet the health-enhancing/
qualities of G-Foods/
Others bemoan the havoc G-Foods
are wreaking on the health of Man and
on environmental health/
Many a calamity has/
befallen mankind on account of G-Foods/

G- Foods/
Friend or Foe? /
Panacea to global hunger? /
No one is so sure about/
the long-term repercussions of G-foods/
Yet the more we speculate about G-foods/
The more illusory they become/

G-Foods, /
Food or Poison? /
That's a thorny question! /

Bushmen

I am a bushman/
fruit of indigenous/
and alien species/
Jah⁶, I am a hybrid creature/

I am a bushman/
Some call me San/
Others brand me Koi-Koi/
Many call me Masarwa.
I couldn't care less! /
What's in a name? /
Jah, I am a Hottentot/

I am a bushman/
My habitat is in the woods/
I feed on roots and back of trees/
I drink from the streams/
With my cupped hands/
I sleep in the grass/
Jah, I am a bushman,
A friend of nature/

I am a bushman/
A Masarwaa/
A San/
A Koi/
A child of both worlds/
Jah, I am a bushman,
Living in communion with nature/
Loathe to domesticate nature/

---

⁶ God

The Tree

The tree/
So small/
And yet so big/
So short/
And yet so tall/

The tree/
A thousand and one adages/
Revolve around you/
The tree of liberty is watered/
With the blood of martyrs/
The apple never falls far/
from the tree/

The tree/
So barren/
And yet so fertile/
The tree is known by its fruit/
As a tree falls so shall it lie/
If you see the forest for the tree/
You bark up the wrong tree/

The tree/
So abiotic/
And yet so biotic/
The family tree/
Genealogy of the great/
And the not-so-great/

The tree/
When one's sibling is on/
The tree top/
One eats the juiciest fruit/
The tree/
Mother of a great/
Many anecdotes/

Lethal Litter

It's an eyesore! /
Streets strewn with cans/
Plastic bags/
Fecal deposits/
Canine carcasses/
paper, peelings/dung/
We are a throw-away nation! /

Seas and oceans a-choking/
With toxic waste/
And oil spills and phosphates/
Marine life endangered/
Aquatic biodiversity on
On brink of extinction/
Yet Man stands arms akimbo watching! /
Rivers and streams suffocating/
Full of fish pregnant with mercury! /
What are we doing to this earth? /
What shall we bequeath to posterity? /
Stop the carnage now! /

Birds of Passage

I am/
A bird of passage/
My name is *hibou*[7]/
Because humans have learned/
to shoot without missing/
I have learned/
to fly without perching/

I am/
A bird of passage/
Wherever I go/
Humans call me bat/
Hermaphrodite bird/
Straddling the bird
And animal worlds/

I am/
A bird of passage/
My name is weaver-bird/
I hop from tree to tree/
In quest of greener pastures/
Strong in my conviction that/
the early bird catches the worm/

---

[7] owl

Tea Leaf

Infinitesimal/
as you are/
Yet interminable/
source of energy/
Day and night you replenish/
My ebbing strength/
with your juice/

Tea leaf/
Source of vitality/
My day breaks with you/
And ends with you/
I shudder to fathom what/
My world would be without you! /

Tea leaf,
My drug of choice/
I owe you a debt of gratitude/
A friend indeed/
for being a friend in need/

Shapes and Colors

This earth/
is replete with a gamut
of shapes /
Some symmetrical/
Others asymmetrical/

This earth/
of full of shapes/
Some gargantuan;
Others lean.
Some proportionate/
Others disproportionate/

This earth/
is filled with colors/
Some bright/
Others dull/
Some attractive;
Others repulsive/
Some pick and span/
Others tell-tale/
All embarked/
on an ego-bouncing trip.

Time and Tide

Time/
Tangible/
Yet so intangible/
Humankind grapples in vain/
with time in an infernal rat race/

Time/
Perceptible/
And yet so elusive,
Breathtaking and fleeting/

Time,
Quantifiable/
Yet not so quantifiable.
Mortals calibrate you in sounds,
Minutes, hours/
days, weeks, and years/
Fleeting!
Immeasurable/
Surreptitious! /
Time and tide/
Wait for no one/

Our Fragile World

Don't kill the world! /
This land is disfigured/
Choking with nauseous gases/
There is hemorrhage/
Streams and rivers festering
with toxic waste.

Don't kill the world/
Landmines abound/
Fields overgrazed/
Forests depleted/
Animal habitats destroyed/
Birds without nests/
Flying helter-skelter/
Let's save the world!

Palm-Wine

Juice of the palm-tree/
Aqua vitae/
For all and sundry/
in the *Ndobo* clan/
Where two or more are gathered/
You are there in their midst/

Palm wine/
Ubiquitous lubricant/
You lubricate our bridal beds/
Ditto for libation grounds/

Wine of the palm/
Friend at night/
Friend in the day/
In times of glee/
In times of gloom/
You are a friend indeed/
from the cradle to the grave/
So great is the sanctity of palm wine/

Red Meat

I've sounded this admonition/
time and again/
I'll do so again/
One man's meat/
May be another man's poison/
Too much of a delicacy/
May turn out to be a disease/
This is common sense/
That is not so common/

One man's glee/
Is another man's gloom/
Think of red meat! /
Ponder the havoc/
it's wreaking on our kith and kin/

Some have grown out of proportion/
on account of red meat! /
Others have become hippopotamuses/
as a result of red meat! /
quite a few have metamorphosed/
into roving mountains due to/
rapacious appetite for red meat! /

Let's consume red meat/
But do so in moderation/

Crawlers

Myriads of our valued
friends are crawlers/
Earthworm/
annelid worm living
and burrowing in the ground/

Millipede/
anthropod having
a long segmented body
and two pairs of legs
on each segment/

Spider/
web-spinning
eight-legged anthropod having
a round unsegmented body/

Ant/
wingless industrious insect
of the hymenopterous family/

Snail/
slow-moving gastropod having
a spiral shell
able to enclose its whole body/

Praying mantis/
insect of the family mantidae,
holding its forelegs in a
position suggestive of prayer/

Turtle/
reptile of the order of chelonia,
encased in a shell of bony plates,
having webbed toes/

A good many of our not
so good friends are crawlers too/

Snake/
long limbless reptile
of the suborder of ophidian/

Lizard/
reptile of the suborder of lacertilia,
having a long body
and tail;
four legs, movable eyelids
and a rough scaly hide/

Gecho/
house lizard having
adhesive feet for climbing
vertical surfaces/

Flip is side is—
These are all friends of nature/

Coconut

The coconut/
is one of earth's/
toughest seeds/
Well equipped to survive/
the travails of life's journey/
This seed is able to accomplish/
an aquatic journey of circa/
ten thousand miles against all odds/

How many of earth's inhabitants /
are like the coconut? /
How soon do we falter and/
succumb to the vagaries of life? /

The coconut/
owes it resilience/
to its protective outer cover/
I wish I were a coconut/

Little Turtle

Once upon a time/
I saw a little turtle/
It was sitting in a box/
It was in a puddle/
It ate mosquitoes/
It snapped at a fly/
It snapped at me/
It caught the fly/
But couldn't catch me! /

[By Winston Vakunta, poet's son]

Snow

I can't wait to see/
The big snow again! /
I've got a snowboard/
I've got snow pants too! /
When the big snow comes/
I'll go flying in the air/
With my snowboard/
I want to make a snowman too/
[By Aristide Vakunta, poet's son]

Showers Of Snow

Snow falls like rain/
It falls like leaves from trees/
Snow is like sand/
It's like birds trying to fly/
Snow is like angels in the sky/
It's like flies trying/
To run away from birds/
Snow is like flies trying to land/

[By Winston Vakunta, poet's son]

White Ants

Might is not size/
The white ant is /
quite minuscule/
Yet in less than no time/
it would demolish a baobab/

Little creatures/
Like big creatures make/
the environment/
Each one has a vital
role to play in the eco-system/

Ostrich

I'm an not an ostrich/
Big swift-running bird/
I don't bury my head in the sand/
In the face of imminent danger/

I'm not an ostrich/
Blind paranoid bird/
I don't pretend to be myopic/
In the face of calamity/

I am not an ostrich/
Bogus bird of passage/
Turning a blind eye/
To nature's cataclysms/
I'm not an ostrich/

Cobweb

A cobweb/
Is a network/
Of threads spun/
By a spider/
From secreted liquid/
It's a trap/
A REAL booby-trap/
For unsuspecting insects of prey/
An insidious entanglement/
For unwary human beings/
Our environment is locked/
In a multitude of cobwebs/

PART TWO
Haiku

Beauty

Nature is pretty
She comes in all shapes and forms
Some bright others not

Trajectory

This journey through Earth
Is like a race through rainstorms
End point is heaven.

Meandering

Hope can rise and fall
Like the sun it is born and
Like the sun it dies

Surfeit

Food sure is a boon
Eaten in moderation
Otherwise a bane

Drops of Love

Love is like raindrops
Showering all and sundry
under the blue sky

Earth's Bounty

Sun rises over
the tall and not so tall trees
Day in day out

Claustrophobia

Night time is no time
Marauders loom large often
putting life at risk.

Honey Bee

The beehive is broken
but we haven't killed the bees
much less the Queen Bee

Life Blood

You may think of trees
as a gift from mother Earth
That is what they are

Requiem

Christmas trees are seen
In every home at Christmas
And then in the trash

Biodiversity

Earth is God's creation
filled with so many colors
Some bright others not

Vagaries

After the sunshine
comes the abundant rainfall
Free for all on Earth

Eco-Crisis

Natural world is
Locked in a collision course
With the human world

Gray Matter

It takes one unknowing
man to destroy a forest
But one town to plant

Tragedy of the Commons

Ecological
Cataclysms know no bounds
They affect many

Despoilers

Environmental
Degradation is man's work
The time to stop it

Climate Change

This global warming
Is far from being a real myth
We are all culprits

Degradation

The more we destroy
The environment the more
We are indigent

Opium

Hard drug is my doom
Seldom think of the havoc
Addiction has wreaked

Spills

Our seas are choking
With oil spills from industries
Time to stop the doom

Scallywags

There are a myriad
Scalawags on this great earth
The beetle is one

Predators

In the animal
Kingdom there's a vendetta
Dog eat dog warfare

Transgender

The animal world
Has its own hermaphrodites
The bat surely is!

Bird Ego

Birds on the ground are
not always humble at all
Peacock is cocky

Rat Race

There's fire at home
Animal and animal
Are locked in a race

Nature's Wrath

Nature can be wild
Volcanoes often erupt/
There are some sea floods

Fossil Fuels

Cars are bedfellows
Alas, their deleterious
Effects are legion

Pollution

Burning fossil fuels
Is the primary source of
Pollution on earth

Green spaces

Urban green spaces
Are ecologically
Good places good to live

Elobi[8]

There are swamp dwellers
On the surface of this earth
Hub of poverty

---

[8] swamp

Altitude

The Earth has its peaks
The Mount Kilimanjaro
Is one great mountain

Winged Neighbors

Earth abounds in flies
The housefly and butterfly
Own a butter house